Conversation Tactics
By Anas Malla

information is without a contract or any type of guarantee assurance.

The trademarks that are used are without any consent, and the publication of the trademark is without permission or backing by the trademark owner. All trademarks and brands within this book are for clarifying purposes only and are the owned by the owners themselves, not affiliated with this document.

Bonus!! FREE E-Book

This great book has a Bonus E-book called "10.5 Tips for Massive Success" you can download the book from my website, Just Click Here. I am honored and grateful to give you this free e-book, and I hope this will really help you to take your life to the next level, you can easy read it after downloading.

Thank you and enjoy reading.

If the links do not work, for whatever reason, you can simply visit my website:

Mastering-life.com/10successtipsbook

Table of Contents

Introduction

I want to thank you and congratulate you for downloading the book "Conversation Tactics!"

This book contains proven steps and strategies on how to become skilled at conversation.

Ever wondered why some people look like they own every conversation they have? Do you dream about becoming a more sociable and likable person that won't be shy of something so simple as approaching a stranger?

I used to be extremely shy. I was afraid of initiating a conversation with my co-workers and friends, let alone with people I don't know. Fortunately, I discovered some bullet-proof conversation tactics that turned me in what I am today – a conversation master!

As someone who has been through all that, I feel that I am competent to guide you through the process and share conversation tactics that will help you improve your skills of talking to other people and, therefore, improve your relationships and your life!

Don't think that this is pure theory. I tried to emphasize practical tips, advices and exercises that will help you become a conversation master.

We will cover everything from the basics to the expert stuff. You will learn how to:

- Overcome shyness when starting a conversation
- Increase your conversation confidence
- Lead memorable conversations
- Move up the ladder at your company by building

relationships with co-workers
And much more!

Thanks again for downloading this book, I hope you enjoy it!

Chapter 1 – How to Start a Conversation

We are going to start from the very beginning. In order to have a conversation, you will need to start one.

You might think that this is the hardest step of the entire process, but you can make it very easy by applying the advice from this chapter.

What You Should Know Before You Start a Conversation

You Are in Control

It is going to be much easier to start a conversation if you feel more confident. Think of it like this, when you are in a meeting in a room full of strangers, the chances are that they feel exactly like you. Hell, they are probably even more shy and self-aware!

How can you become more confident that you can start a conversation? Begin by talking to your friends and people you already know. See how easy it is to initiate a conversation with them? Then why do you think it's going to be harder with strangers?

Your goal should be to look outgoing, confident and cool. Believe that you are a master of starting a conversation. That's what all other alpha males (and females) do.

Turn That Frown Upside Down

You've surely heard that body language plays a major role in how people react to you. That is completely true. Three things you want to apply in any situation are:

- Always smile
- Maintain a good posture
- Don't keep your arms crossed

By applying these, you will send a message that you are confident, secure and approachable. You'll also appear cheerful, and who doesn't like people with a jolly spirit? Be careful, I'm not saying laugh out loud at a business meeting. Adjust your attitude in accordance where you are, but make sure not to look frowned.

Let's take a look at the results of a survey conducted in the United States. When asked what's the friendliest thing a person can do when meeting a stranger, 87% of people answered – SMILE.

If you think about it, it makes sense. When you scan a room full of people, those with a smile on their face will look more like a conversation material than the ones wearing a frown.

Politeness Goes a Long Way

It's nothing new that you need to be polite, but I'm talking about adjusting your behavior to the social situation you are currently in. A polite approach in business means that you should introduce yourself and shake hands with the other person(s). On the other hand, you might skip this at a party and start the conversation with a witty remark. Of course, you should always make sure not to be interruptive or rude.

Studies show that it takes only 5 seconds for a person to form an impression about you. That impression if finalized within the first minute and it is very hard to change it afterward. That is why you need to show the nicest and best part of you for a first impression.

Stay Focused

Don't think that the job is over once you pull through the introduction line. Make sure to listen carefully what your conversation partner has to say in reply. Stay focused and don't wander around with your eyes. You need to send a message that you are interested in having the conversation. Furthermore, carefully listening to what the other side has to say might provide an opportunity to continue the conversation.

Use Your Detective Skills

If you want to approach a stranger, observing him might provide you with topics for starting a conversation.

Imagine that you are at a party. Notice what the other person drinks and initiate a discussion about that drink. If you are at a business meeting, you can always use business topics to start a conversation.

Real-Life Examples

Let's discuss some examples from real life that can help you find a way to start a conversation

Talking to a Stranger

They say that if changes of the weather don't exist, 90% of the people wouldn't have anything to talk about.

"Such a nice day, right?"

That is NOT a good conversation starter. It doesn't lead to additional questions and a meaningful conversation.

So, what you should talk about?

The important thing to know here is that people LOVE to

talk about themselves. You need to find a conversation starter that will allow your partner to express their opinion.

If you are in a big room full of people, you can use something like:

"Hi, I'm Michael. I'm still not entirely comfortable with this big group of people. How are you handling the situation?"

Not only you asked the other side to talk about themselves, but you also asked for help, which is also a great conversation starter.

Talking at Business Meetings

In any social situations related to business, always keep the hierarchy in mind. There is a big difference between talking to your superiors and inferiors. Regardless of your conversation partner, make sure to keep your focus on the final goal of the discussion.

You want to be kind to your employees, but you also want to look like their leader at all times. On the other hand, if the conversation partner is your superior, make sure to show respect for them. That doesn't mean you should be frightened but always acknowledge their position.

I assume you are most interested in how to ask your boss for a salary raise. Never start with a direct question. Instead, ask for an opinion on your performance. Depending on the answer, you might ask for a raise immediately or explain that you will try to improve your performance in the future to deserve it.

Talking at Parties or in Bars

Make sure to look as approachable as you can (refer back to the "Turn That Frown Upside Down" section for advice) and pay attention to detail. The easiest way to start a conversation at a party is to focus on a detail. If the person you want to approach is having an alcoholic drink, initiate a conversation about that. After asking about his/her favorite drink, you can continue the conversation by talking about the party. Talk about the music or other people there. Asking additional questions will help you keep the flow of the conversation.

Chapter 2 – How to Overcome Shyness

There are different kinds of shyness when it comes to talking to people. Some have a problem with anxiety whenever they need to attend a meeting or be in a large crowd. Others are afraid to say anything because they are scared of embarrassing themselves. Both of these may influence your abilities to start a conversation or keep it going.

Do you consider yourself a shy person?

The good news is that it's not genetic. It's not something you were born with and cannot repair. Being shy is just a pattern of emotions, behavior, and thoughts we display in social situations.

It's a matter of habit.

Correct, you are shy only because you've adapted to the world that way. There are tips and things you can do to overcome shyness, but first things first.

Identify the Problem

The initial step should be to realize what patterns of shyness you exhibit. Are you afraid of attending a meeting or you are frightened if someone tries to talk to you there? Are you scared of talking to strangers or you hate to be a part of a group discussion?

Either way, think about how these reasons are not rational. Remember how we discussed making yourself more approachable in the first chapter of this book? Freshen your memory if need be and take a look at those rules again as they especially apply if you are shy.

The trick is in making yourself being used to different social situations. Take a look at some tips you can apply to overcome your shyness

Tips to Overcome Shyness

Engage in Different Situations

The easiest way to overcome shyness is to be in as much different social situations as you can. Instead of shutting yourself at home, go out and get surrounded by people. You can go to the movies or the local race track, pretty much anywhere where it's crowded. If you go alone, not only you will get used to people being around you but you will also feel much more comfortable talking to strangers. Of course, if you apply the conversation tactics you find throughout this book.

Refrain from Negative Thinking

You are probably hesitant to talk to other people because you are afraid that you will say something dumb. There is absolutely no reason for this!

I mean, ask yourself – what's the worst it could happen? Is it that you can make a mistake? You can always apologize for it. That is the worst-case scenario of you walking to other people.

When you put it like that, it doesn't sound scary. Whatever mistake that you make, you can always apologize and try turning it into a joke. You can even use it in open a door to a conversation.

Don't let negative thoughts about what can go wrong affect the quality of your conversation. If you think positively, you will react much better to current circumstances and be more confident that you can handle any discussion.

Talk to Different People Every Day

Think about giving yourself a simple task every day. It may range from talking to at least one stranger every day to simpler things like entering the office and wishing everyone good morning. Try talking to a co-worker you don't usually engage with. Compliment his/her outfit or simply ask how their day is going. It would be a problem doing this the first couple of times. Once you get ahold of it, it will become a piece of cake and you will be wondering was there a need to be shy in the first place.

Shy persons often think that they don't have anything smart to say or that they simply don't know how to make so-called small talk. Talking to new people will increase your confidence and your social behavior will elevate to a higher level.

If you think you have a problem with small talk, I've prepared you a list of questions you may ask depending on the topic:

Work – in most cases, you will use these topics when talking to a co-worker:

- How long have you been working here?
- Are you satisfied with what you do? Would you like to change your career?
- What college did you go to?

Family – people like talking about themselves and, therefore, their family:

- Do you have any brothers or sisters?
- Are you married or have a boyfriend/girlfriend?

- Do you have any kids?

Recreation – perhaps the most interesting subject for most people. It offers a broad range of topics, including:

- What are your favorite sports?
- Are you a movie fan? What's your favorite genre?
- What kind of music do you like?

These are just several questions, so you can get the idea of what you can talk about. The important thing to note is that you need to adjust questions to the environment and to the conversation partner.

For example, you might have heard that your co-worker recently had a baby. A good thing to ask is:

"How you are feeling as a new parent?"

If you are at a party, aside from asking about the general kind of music your conversation partner likes, you can also ask:

"Do you like this DJ?"

The goal is to ask open-ended questions and ones that can keep the conversation going. You can start by asking:

"Are you a movie fan?"

This is a great way to start a conversation about movies in general. We are all fans of movies, so you can continue discussing favorite genres or actors and the latest box office hits.

Make sure to listen to what your conversation partner has to say. If he/she says that she likes comedy movies, that's where you need to take the conversation. Don't think that small talk is just coming up with good questions. It's also about listening to what the other side has to say and offering your own opinions.

Chapter 3 – How to Leave a Good Impression During the Conversation

I mentioned before that the first impression is crucial to what a person will think about you. That is why it is extremely important to leave a good impression during the first conversation you have with someone.

Some people think that people are likable because of some trait they have. For example, they suppose that handsome guys and girls are likable because they are handsome. That is as far from the truth as it can be.

We have to admit that some characteristics might contribute to a person being more likable. However, there is no much use in being handsome if you are obsessed with yourself. Narcissistic people often talk only about themselves which is why they usually don't leave a good impression and bore people around them quickly.

The good news is that there are conversation tactics that can help you leave a good impression during any conversation you might have:

Conversation Tactics for Leaving a Good Impression

Keep Smiling

Nobody likes people that don't know anything else but to complain. Instead, we all look for those who can make us smile and cheer us up when we are down. When you are at a social event, make sure to put your worries aside and be positive.

The Importance of Body Language

We talked that body language has a major role to play in leaving a good impression. So, how to use it to your advantage?

Don't keep your arms crossed and maintain a good posture. Your hands should be relaxed and you shouldn't wander around with your eyes. You want to look like you are interested in what the other party has to say.

Listen Carefully

Aside from looking like you want to listen to the other party, make sure that you actually hear what they have to say.

There are some physical signs you can use to show that you are paying attention. For example, nod your head in agreement when you think it's fitting or motivate the other party to continue the story by asking a good question (more on that later).

Get in Touch with the Latest Events

There are two areas to focus on here:

- Current global and local events
- Specific events related to the environment

Keeping yourself informed about the global events doesn't mean that you should know each and every piece of news. Simply make sure to know the trending events everyone is talking about and you should be good to go.

Now let's focus on the latter one. Staying in touch with environment-related events means that, if you are at work, you should know what's going on with your co-workers.

We can use the example of your co-worker recently having a baby again. That information is an excellent conversation starter to use with everyone around the office.

Use the Name of the Other Party

Believe it or not, people love to hear their own names. Use this simple trick to strengthen your relationship with anyone. When you address people by their name, you make sure that they will listen. Plus, they feel like they are important enough that you memorized their name. On top of that, you can also give a more casual atmosphere to the conversation by addressing the other party directly.

There is one thing to note here – if you are at a formal event, you should always make sure to check if the other party agrees with you calling them by their name.

Ask Good Questions

I've already mentioned this and there will be a whole chapter on this issue, so you can see that it is a pretty important one. There is no better way to show your interest than to ask questions. You should make sure to find the balance; you don't want to be boring or make it seem like you are constantly interrupting.

If your conversation partner has just started what seems to be a long story, it's a good idea to ask a question every now and then. It will show him/her that you are listening to the story carefully.

Questions are also a way of continuing the conversation. If the other party has finished talking about something, you can ask a question on the topic to hear more details about it.

If you are scared that you are troubling the other party with constant questions, don't hesitate to ask something along the lines of:

"Am I boring you with my questions?"

Don't Be Rude

And by rude, I mean – don't be judgmental. I'm sure that you wouldn't like someone you just met to pass judgment on your actions. You would consider it rude and you would be right.

That is why you should be polite if you and the other party have a different point of views on certain things. The best thing to do is to move the conversation in another direction and steer clear of any further discussion.

Honesty Is the Best Policy

You should always be honest when talking to other people. Nobody expects you to like everything, it's perfectly normal to have your own opinion on things. Believe it or not, people will respect you more if you disagree politely and offer a different point of view.

Keep in mind one thing – human mind works in mysterious ways. Being honest doesn't mean that you should say everything that strikes your mind. It just means that you can say if you have a different opinion of something than the other party.

Let's see an example. Your female co-worker might ask you about how you like her new hairstyle. You actually don't like it at all, but you know you have to be polite. Instead of hurting her feelings, offer an alternative answer such as:

"It really brings out your eyes."

By using that answer, you both answered honestly and protected her feelings.

Use Compliments

Compliments also have their own chapter, meaning that they are very important. We all love getting a compliment. They even say that people don't care what you are complimenting as long as you say something nice of them.

The one thing you want to make sure is not to overuse compliments. Make them honest, unique and seldom. Focus on a detail you really like on a person. For example, compliment your co-worker's earrings. If the compliment is sincere, it will sound much better and will have a better effect.

Use Physical Contact

It might seem weird at first, but it's actually a great way of strengthening your connection with other people. We make physical contact all the time. When we introduce ourselves – we shake hands. When we want someone to turn around – we tap them on a shoulder.

Don't be afraid to use physical contact to make a connection with the other party, but be very careful and don't overuse it.

Chapter 4 – How to Recognize High Points of a Conversation

Have you ever listened to a politician holding a public speech? He/she usually tells a whole lot of sentences, but only small portion of them deserve an applause.

We can say that it's the same with any conversation. All discussions have their low and high points. High points are exactly what they sound like – the best part of a conversation. I'm talking about those moments where you clearly share a connection, moments that stay as the most memorable part of the conversation.

Conversations are like waves and they will fluctuate between low and high points. All that you need to do is to recognize those points and capitalize on them. Many people don't acknowledge when they reach a high point in a conversation and fail to use them to make an even stronger emotional bond.

Yes, high points have a lot to the with emotions. A high point can be sharing a laugh when you tell a nice joke, for example.

When you share a laugh with your conversation partner, both of you feel great. The problem appears when the conversation starts oscillating back from that high point. In some cases, the energy recedes so deep that both parties lose interest in having a conversation.

What we want to use as a conversation tactics is how to use the change of energy during a conversation to our advantage.

How to Recognize High Points?

If you want to utilize the high point, you have to learn how to recognize one. There is one thing that you need to focus on – emotions.

During a conversation, some things will not make you feel anything, while other topics will cause a strong reaction for both you and the other party. If you experience a strong emotion during a conversation, the chances are you've reached a high point.

It can be anything of the following:

- Sharing a laugh
- Sharing a sad emotion
- Sharing a strong perspective on a certain issue

Basically, a high point is anything that makes a strong mental connection between the two parties participating in a conversation.

How to Use High Points?

Once you've recognized a high point, the important thing is to remember it. It can be of great use in future conversations. You can even use it as a conversation starter when you see that person next time. There are certain tricks you can use when you want to refer to a previous high-point again.

Let's see an example:

You created a high point by making a joke that you look like Dumbo because of your big ears. Then to conversation continued and you've reached the topic of wearing hats and other accessories. You've managed to brilliantly connect the two topics by saying:

"I could never wear a baseball cap because I would look even more like Dumbo."

By doing this, you've created a new high point while referring to a previous one.

What exactly do you get by using the same high points multiple times?

First, it shows that you paid attention and listened to the other party. Furthermore, it's not that easy to use a high point that appeared in a completely different topic, so your conversation partner will also think that you are clever and witty. Finally, you're strengthening the bond you made when you created the high point in the first place.

I will try to explain in a more understanding way by giving another example. During a conversation, a high point occurred where both you and the other party expressed your hatred for lack of available parking spots throughout of the city. In the meantime, it started raining and the other party steered the conversation in that direction. That is the perfect moment to say:

"The rain is going to make it even tougher to find available parking spots."

If you apply the use of high points, chances are that you can stop the conversation from oscillating too much in terms of energy and interest. It's a great conversation tactic to keep the discussion going with as much spark as possible. Aside from that, you're leaving an impression that you are a likable and smart person and a very interesting conversation partner.

Another thing to pay attention to is that the other party doesn't figure out what you are doing. Once you get ahold of using high points, you are on your way to mastering your ability to lead a great conversation.

Chapter 5 – How to Ask the Right Questions During a Conversation

High points are one way of keeping a conversation going. Another, equally or more important, item on that list is asking the right questions.

What makes any conversation great is that both parties actively participate and contribute to it. It's important to create a good flow for the conversation and allow the other party to express their opinion.

Questions that add value to the conversation and keep its flow are also called invitations. Keep in mind that we don't consider all questions to be invitations. There are two things that a question needs to fulfill in order to become an invitation:

- Let the other party know that it's their turn to talk
- Let the other party know what should they talk about

So, what would be an example of an invitational question?

"I left the work earlier today. What happened after I left?"

This question clearly lets your conversation partner know that it is his/her turn to talk and you are providing them a topic to talk about.

Invitational questions are your way out of silences during a conversation. If you believe that you've exhausted your current topic, you can expand it by asking an invitational question. Alternatively, invitations can also serve as a great tool to steer the conversation in a completely different direction. It's not necessary for the question to be connected with the current topic if you think that the topic is not fitting. Simply use an invitation to change it!

The Importance of Open-Ended Questions

There are two types of questions. "Yes or no" questions are the first type and you want to avoid them at all cost. Why? Because they are "closed-ended".

"Did you have a good vacation?"

When you ask this, the other party can simply answer with "Yes" or "No" and you don't want that. Instead, you want them to open up and talk more about their vacation. You don't want to settle for a one-word response.

Now let's take a look at the exactly same question asked in a different way:

"What did you do during your vacation?"

The objective is the same – you want the person to talk about their vacation. However, this way you invite them to talk about what happened to them during the holiday. This question is called "open-ended" because it can't be answered with a simple "Yes" or "No". Instead, it's a clear invitation to share and keeps the conversation going.

When you ask an open-ended question, you will notice the magic happening in no time. The other party believes that you are genuinely interested in how they spent their vacation and they immediately start sharing their memories.

Asking insightful questions helps you to leave a good impression. It strengthens the relationship you formed with the other party and shows that you really care about them.

How to Ask the Right Questions?

It's not an easy job to come up with a right question and ask it at the perfect moment. There are two things to avoid here:

- Asking extremely superficial questions that won't allow you to find out anything about the other person:
  "Do you think that the weather will be nice tomorrow?"

- Asking extremely intimate questions that go way out of the comfort level of the other party:
  "What's your deepest, darkest secret?"

It all comes down to how good you know a person. If it's your first conversation with someone, it is a good idea to start with superficial questions. An example of a good question can be:

"What's your favorite thing about dogs?"

After that, you slowly build up and strengthen the mental connection with the other party and move on to deeper questions. Of course, make sure to avoid extremely intimate questions, except if you are a very good friend with that person.

When you initiate a conversation with a stranger, you can always start with the question about the weather if you can't come up with anything better. However, try to move on to the next level as quickly as possible. Questions about work come to mind as a natural next step as they are a bit intimate, but they probably won't scare your conversation partner.

Pay attention to the comfort level of the other party. If they don't seem comfortable with answering your question, you went in too deep. If they express comfort in answering your questions, feel free to continue digging.

"What's your dream job?"

"What's your perfect vacation destination?"

These are examples of questions that are pretty deep but probably won't trouble the other side.

An example to keep in mind that it takes a long period of time to establish trust. It's impossible to move on from the questions about whether to the darkest secrets over the course of a single conversation. You will need to have dozens or hundreds of conversations before you ask a very intimate question.

As every conversation goes by, the opportunity for more and more intimate questions will show up. Don't forget that any relationship is a two-way street. If you want people to share intimate things about themselves, you have to offer something in return. That means that you should also expect intimate questions and you should be prepared to answer them honestly. In order to build a strong connection, both parties should open up.

We are finishing this chapter the same way as we finished the previous one. If you want to become a master at conversation tactics, the important thing is that the other participants don't figure out your game.

It's the same with invitational questions. They are a good way to build rapport with the other party, but you should make sure that the flow of conversation feels natural.

Don't make it awkward by asking too many invitational questions. The other participant might feel like he is in an interview instead of a conversation. If there is a silence in a conversation and you believe that the topic is exhausted, feel free to use an explicit invitational question. On the other hand, keep in mind the conversation flow and make sure it all seems natural.

Chapter 6 – How to Use the Two-Second Tactic

I mentioned in the previous chapters that people like talking about themselves. That couldn't be truer. The reason why we all love this is because we just love being heard. When somebody is listening to what we have to say, we feel like we matter.

It's not that we like to brag (although, there is nothing wrong with that). The thing is – people need validation. We are all looking for others to validate who we are and what we do.

People love being in the spotlight. Even those that say they don't like talking about themselves usually do that because they've not established an adequate level of trust with others and are afraid that they will receive criticism instead of validation.

There's another interesting thing. Ever heard someone saying "they stole my thunder?" When somebody is in the center of attention, others that feel neglected will try to take the spotlight away from them. Some people are craving for attention so much that they always try to make the story about them.

A good conversation involves the spotlight going back and forth, just like the ball in a tennis match. You should share your opinions and experience, especially if the other party asks you to, but you should also make sure to attentively listen to what they have to say.

When the other participant is talking, make sure to let them know that you listen. Don't make a mistake by rudely interrupting them and jumping in as soon as they finish their sentence (interrupting politely is an entirely different conversation tactic that we will cover later in the book).

It is considered rude to speak as soon as the other party stopped talking,

Why?

Because your conversation partner will have an impression that you couldn't wait for them to finish and you didn't even listen attentively. You will look too eager to start talking yourself and like you didn't care about what the other party had to say.

Fortunately, conversation experts have a solution for this. We call it a two-second tactic.

What Is a Two-Second Tactic?

The rule is actually pretty self-explanatory. It means that you should wait for two seconds before saying anything after the other party finishes talking. This is especially important if the other participant was speaking for a longer period of time or about something that is considered personal.

Why should you do that?

The reason is simple – it will appear like you are acknowledging what your conversation partner has just said. Two seconds is considered an appropriate amount of time to soak in the information you got.

You can try counting two seconds in your head. Of course, an important thing to note is that you should actually appear like you are soaking in what the person just said. People will look at you looking for signs if you were listening. Your facial expression should not be a simple blank stare. Instead, you should look like that you are thinking about the information you just got.

Benefits of the Two-Second Tactic

You might think that you have a perfect reply or a comment to continue the conversation going. In most cases, you simply can't wait to seize the spotlight and say the perfect comment. A wiser thing to do is to wait for two seconds as it will increase your likability.

Applying a two-second wait rule before replying will also create a moment of tension in the conversation. You will not only send a message that you are genuinely interested and that you were attentively listening. You will also communicate power and confidence of a real conversation master.

Yes, two seconds is all it takes to convince people that you were listening to them with attention. We all love to be heard when we are talking. Two seconds seem like a short span of time, but it's just enough to send a message that you've actually given a thought about what the other party said before you offered a reply. You will make yourself a valuable participant in the conversation by making the other participant a valuable part of the discussion.

In some cases, you can even make a mistake. When telling a longer story, people can occasionally make a short pause. This pause does not mean that they are finished speaking. Instead, they just took a little break. Imagine if you jumped in and interrupted them with your comment, even though their story hasn't been finished. It would immediately decrease your likability and you would be considered rude.

Not to mention that they will think if you have enough respect for them and if you even care what they have to say.

As you can say, two seconds can make a big difference in what kind of impression you will leave. That is why you should make sure to apply this conversation tactic and send the right message.

How to Fill the Two Seconds?

"Wow, that's interesting!"

This is an example of a sentence you can use to fill the two-second void to your reply. Beware of one thing – if you do this too often, it can get annoying. Your conversation partner might also think that you just used the sentence to stop them talking and seize the spotlight for yourself.

There is a much better way.

Think about waiting for two seconds and then starting your response with saying "that's interesting." Believe it or not, conversation experts have come to a conclusion that this improves the effect of the two-second tactic. By combining the two, you will show the other party that you acknowledged what they had to say and show your appreciation for it.

Chapter 7 – How to Interrupt Politely

Your parents probably taught you that interrupting someone when they are speaking is rude. I'm sure they've had a good intention, but guess what? They taught you wrong!

Although not entirely wrong. Constant interrupting is rude and it sends the wrong message to other people. If you always interrupt them, they will think that you are self-absorbed and might even start secretly hating you. Who can blame them if you are constantly interrupting when they are trying to say something?

So, the truth is somewhere in the middle. Often interrupting will lead you to break the connection you have formed with the other party up to that point. On the other side, there are some great benefits to reap if you learn how to interrupt politely.

Before we start with some tactics on how to interrupt someone in a polite way, let me warn you:

Please read this chapter with caution!

Mastering the art of polite interrupting is not easy. There is a fine line between strengthening the relationship and stepping on someone's toes by interrupting them.

Okay, now that is out of the way, let's see how to find that fine line and walk it like an artist.

Why You Should Interrupt Only to Agree

There are moments where you seem intrigued by what the other party has been saying. They seem to be completely in line with the opinion you have on a certain topic. You are so excited about that that you simply cannot hold it in!

In these cases, it's completely fine to interrupt someone to agree with them. There is an additional bonus if you can complete the other party's sentence as it will truly show them that you've brought your emotions into the conversation.

Let's see an example:

The other party: "I was just on a business trip in Los Angeles and I loved it there when..."

You: "...Really? That's unbelievable, I used to live in Los Angeles and it is my favorite city in the whole world!"

Notice how the interruption used the emotions of the other party for Los Angeles to strengthen the bond with them.

Here's another illustration:

The other party: "The Saw was just such an amazing movie. I was thrilled with all of it, but I especially liked..."

You: "...the ending? Oh, my God, it was such a shocker for me, too!"

This example also shows that you are excited about what the other party has to say. The excitement is on a such a high level that you can't wait for them to finish and you must interrupt them.

The point is that there is a point in why you are interrupting. You are not just making a random interruption to babble something about yourself. Instead, you show that you are emotionally engaged in the conversation and that you completely agree with the other person.

We all like when someone agrees with us. That is why you should use the moment when you reach that spot where you are at the same emotional place with the other party and interrupt them to agree.

Who doesn't like others to agree with them, especially in these modern times where people often get isolated and alienated? Humans are social beings and feeling like they are similar to you creates a strong emotional bond. You not only agree, you reach a deep and honest understanding.

As with other conversation tactics, don't overdo it as it is impossible to be emotionally identical to the other party. Be honest and don't use dirty tactics like learning how to predict someone's sentences.

You can easily notice when it is the perfect time to interrupt. Your conversation partner will look excited and worked up about his story. He/she might even use hyperbole or big proclamations.

If you feel strongly about what they are saying at that moment, interrupt them!

Let's see another example you can use:

The other party: "I love laptops and tablets. I cannot believe that that guy over there is using a PC. It's so..."

You: "...old-fashioned, right. Why can't he just buy Apple iPad? They have such great products!"

There are two ways to go here – one is to use the information you have discovered during previous discussions with a client.

Another option is to guess. Of course, here you are facing the danger of your interruption backfiring. There's always a chance that the other party doesn't love Apple's products (or anything else you used in your interruption). If you miss and use something that your conversation partner does not like, you also miss an opportunity to strengthen the bond.

Allow Them to Interrupt

A hidden tactic gem that you can use here is reversing the process. Instead of interrupting the other party, allow them to interrupt you.

"Check it out, a desktop computer! I cannot believe it! They are so…"

Stop there and allow them to pick up. They will have the option of answering that desktop computers are great or that they hate them. Either way, you will know where to take the conversation further.

Chapter 8 – How to Give and Receive Compliments

There is a saying that people will believe everything you tell them as long as it's a compliment. This is not true, although we all love getting compliments for both our looks and personality.

The effect of compliments, however, depends on your ability to properly communicate them. Some people are natural talents for giving compliments, while others need some exercise.

The important thing to know that compliments are most effective when they are sincere. You should avoid offering general compliments, such as:

"You look great today!"

While it is a nice sentence, it sounds a bit superficial. It would have a greater effect if you made a particular observation.

"Are those new earrings? They go great with your style!"

Compliments should be unique and you also need to pay attention to communicate them in a proper tone. In other words, you need to make them look believable. Use a meaningful tone of voice and always keep a sincere smile.

So, what should you compliment people on? Let's take a look at some ideas on:

How to Give the Perfect Compliment?

Always Compliment What the Other Party Likes

This will require knowing a thing or two about the other party, but it will prove extremely fruitful. The truth is that people often give compliments on stuff they consider to be important. They don't wonder what is important for the other party. A sure-fire way to find out about what your conversation partner likes is to ask them.

Compliment Personal Qualities

Personality traits are one thing that you should always look to praise. It can be anything from attention to detail to politeness, warmth, and friendliness. This type of compliments goes a longer way than praising skills people have learned, such as project management or public speaking.

Focus on More Than Just Appearance

It's not that you shouldn't praise a person's appearance, but the goal should be for the compliment to strengthen the relationship with the other party on a deeper, more emotional level. Say something like:

"I know fitting into this company wasn't an easy job for you, but I can see that you managed to get through it."

This way, you included emotions in your compliment and you recognized the person for who they are. Your praise didn't just seem like off-the-shelf compliment you reached to be polite, but it seems like you genuinely thought about your praise and took an interest in the other party.

Focus on efforts, accomplishments and personality traits.

They have a much better power of boosting the other party's self-confidence than simply praising their appearance.

Use One Detail

In other words – be specific. General compliments usually look like you haven't tried at all. If your co-worker decided to decorate the office with flowers, you have two options to praise them:

"Nice flowers!"

"Beautiful flowers! I love how you created so much texture with only one flower color!"

As you can see, the other option is much better as it makes the compliment more personal and directed.

Don't Have a Hidden Agenda

The compliments have the best effect when you deliver them for no particular reason (except, of course, being kind or wanting to praise the other person). The perfect compliment shouldn't have a hidden agenda and shouldn't have an obvious benefit for the provider. It should also be respectful, sincere and given at the right moment.

Why You Should End with a Question

Some people are not good at receiving compliments. They might be too shy and an awkward silence may occur after your praise. For that reason, consider ending your compliment by asking them a question.

"Your hair looks amazing. Do you use a conditioner or some other product?"

By ending your praise with a question, you give your party an option on what they can say. Plus, it additionally emphasizes your sincere interest in the topic.

How to Properly Receive Compliments

Sometimes it is much easier to give a compliment than to properly receive it. There might be various reasons why you have problems accepting a compliment that another person is offering. You might be shy or you might be having confidence issues causing you to think that you are not worthy of praise. Keep in mind that this is far from the truth. If another person thinks that you deserve a compliment, then the chances are that you really deserve a compliment!

What are some of the wrong ways to react to a compliment coming your way?

"Anybody could do it."

"Oh, come on, it's nothing."

Yes, it might seem like you are humble and modest, but in reality, you have troubles with confidence. While modesty is among the best personality traits anyone can have, there are times when you should acknowledge your accomplishments and be proud of them. These moments are those when other people also acknowledge them.

Additionally, think about the message you are sending with this type of reply. It seems like you are dismissing or diminishing the compliment that the other person has given you. It's like you say that it doesn't mean much to you. It might even seem that you consider the praise dishonest. But when you get a compliment, it actually means that someone has shared their opinion about you. They showed genuine interest in you and the best you can do is to put in a little more effort in replying. In other cases, the other party might just praise you to be polite, but that still doesn't mean you should try to properly answer their compliment.

In most cases, it's your shyness and lack of confidence that prevent you from responding to a praise in a proper manner. If your initial reaction is awkward silence or blushing, let's take a look at some conversation tactics you can apply:

Respond with a Thank You

The initial response to every praise should be the old, simple "thank you". If you know a person better, you can expand the sentence with something like:

"Thank you, I appreciate that, especially coming from you."

This is a good way to, for example, emphasize that you appreciate the compliment about your hairstyle coming from a friend who is into fashion trends.

Alternatively, you can emphasize that a certain job project wasn't an easy job for you and you are glad that it went well:

"Thank you, I've really put great effort into this project. I'm glad my co-workers noticed it."

Feel Free to Blush

First of all, blushing is sort of a physical or a chemical reaction. It means that you don't have great control over it. Don't be ashamed that you blushed because of the praise you just received. Instead, use it to your advantage:

"Thank you, your praise is making me blush."

It's a great way to do two things:

- Reduce your inner tension
- Let the other person know that you appreciate the compliment

Keep Your Smile On

If we are smiling, we are happy about something. When you smile while you receive a compliment, it means that you are happy that you are on the receiving end of it. A smile on your face adds extra effect to your response in which you will show appreciation for the praise.

Smiling is also important because people relate it to confidence. If you smile when you are getting a compliment, it means that you are confident about your personality traits and skills.

Use It to Continue the Conversation

A compliment may be a way into the next topic of the conversation. Never forget to show appreciation and thank the other party for the compliment. After that, you can use it to keep the conversation flow going.

Let's take a look at an example:

"I love your hair!"

We've talked about how it's always better to end the compliment with a question. Not all people are conversation masters, so they might leave out the question part. Regardless, you might act liked they asked you something related to the compliment. In this case, you can answer how you got the idea for your new hairstyle:

"Thank you, I appreciate that coming from you. I was watching TV and saw that popular movie star (insert name), so I was trying to look more like him/her. Did I succeed?"

Don't Compliment Back

At least don't do it immediately. We mentioned that

receiving a compliment is like getting an opinion about yourself. If you respond with a praise, it won't have much effect. It will probably look that you are faking it in an effort to be nice. Instead, wait for a little while and insert your compliment during the rest of the conversation.

Chapter 9 – How to Use Humor in a Conversation

There is a famous story about the American president Abraham Lincoln that gives a nice picture of using the effects of humor to your advantage. When an opponent said that Lincoln is two-faced, the president answered:

"Do you think that I would be wearing this face if I have two of them?"

His reply laughed the audience and strengthen his connection with them.

Another metaphor is to think about humor as a lubricant for social situations. It is a way of keeping the conversation smooth.

Humor is very effective to use in a conversation. There is a lot that it can do, including:

- Strengthen your bond with other people, including friends, co-workers, and customers
- Create high points in a conversation
- Make tough conversations less difficult
- Reduce tension and deflect criticism and anger
- Allow you to share your point of view

It's also effective in working environments, where it also can:

- Remove barriers among people, such as superiors and inferiors
- Motivate employees and boost their morale

- Stimulate problem-solving
- Manage conflicts and reduce frustration

Humor is a priceless conversation tactic that can bring you many benefits. However, not all people are skilled at using humor to their advantage. Let's take a look at some tips you can use to get better at using it:

Tips on Using a Humor

Humor Is Not a Weapon

Sharp humor might hurt others. Yes, some people might appreciate dark or offensive humor, but those people are very rare. That is why offensive humor should stay in stand-up comedy shows and other places where it is appropriate to use it.

The first thing to remember if you want to use humor in a conversation is that humor can also be damaging if you:

- Laugh at someone
- Use offensive humor

There are some personal and controversial topics you should avoid, such as religion, race, appearance, weight and so on. The best thing to do is to completely steer clear of these topics. You might consider that you are just teasing someone about their weight, but they might think that you are offending them or it may be a huge blow to their confidence. It's very easy for this type of humor to backfire and rupture your relationship.

Never use humor as a weapon that will do harm and point out the deficiencies of others. Instead, it should be a tool that will help you strengthen the bond with the other party by laughing with them.

Leave Your Pride at Home

Unlike laughing at others, laughing at yourself is allowed and acceptable in a conversation. I always go to performances of this over-weight stand-up comedian because I know his best jokes will be about his extra pounds (I was also a bit overweight, so I can relate).

Conan O'Brien, the famous TV host, is a great example of a person that directs jokes at himself. He and other experts at self-deprecating humor agree that if you are ready to laugh at yourself, you will never lack material for making jokes.

During a conversation, loosen things up by telling a story how you had a "bad hair day", how you felt when you were the only man in a conference room full of women or anything like that. Of course, keep it tasteful, it doesn't mean that you should humiliate yourself.

Use Humor to Reduce Tension

There are points in a discussion where you can simply cut the tension. Let's consider this example that an anonymous author shared online:

"I was four years old and my mom took me to work because he couldn't leave me at home. I started meeting people around her office and, when the boss came in, I was shocked. She had a pretty memorable look – hooked nose, long pointy chin and dark hair.

Considering that I was a kid, I had to say: "Mom, she looks like an evil witch!" I can't describe the awkward silence that occurred. My mom tried to control the situation by saying: "You think Glenda the Good Witch from the Wizard of Oz?"

I knew who Glenda, so I replied:

"Nooo, Glenda was pretty!"

That brought the tension to a whole new level. Fortunately, my mother's boss knew how important humor was to reduce the tension. She laughed and others started laughing."

As you can see, humor can be used at stressful points during a conversation and is especially efficient if you combine it with the previous tip of laughing at yourself.

Don't Go Off-Topic

Jokes you use should be related to the conversation are currently leading. If your humor is irrelevant, it won't have a good effect. You either won't get a reaction or simply get a polite smile. In most cases, the other participants in the discussion will think that the person telling the joke is just craving for attention. You can rehearse some stories to use as humorous, but you also need to recognize the perfect spot to insert them. As you become more experienced and skilled in leading the conversation flow, you will be more able to steer the conversation in the way you need it to go for your humorous story.

Another good trick is to have a story connected to each piece of your clothing. As soon as someone gives you a compliment or notices a particular part of your attire, you will have an interesting story prepared to tell them.

How to Become Better at Humor

They say that analyzing humor is like dissecting a frog. Not many people are interested and the frog dies of it. Nonetheless, I'll try to explain to you how to become better at humor.

Understand How to Use Punchlines

A punchline is a sentence that finished the joke and it is intended to make people laugh. The key to making a good punchline is to offer a twist. You need to offer your listeners something that will surprise them, perhaps even at a moment when they least expect it:

"The hardest thing about the death of my grandmother was…making it look like an accident"

You've felt that the discussion reached that serious point where you need to reduce the tension. The first part of the sentence was a so-called "set up" and the latter part is the punchline.

Let's divide it. This is a set-up:

"Did you hear about the new survey that claims that women are in charge of cleaning 67% of the households?"

You can use the set-up while you are talking about anything related to cleaning. The punchline comes afterward:

"The rest of the houses are dirty."

Make a Witty Response

You can also look for opportunities to make a witty response. For example, I go to the gym regularly but I'm not that dedicated to exercising. When I stretch, I usually spend 2 minutes actually stretching and 8 minutes talking to people in the room. When one of them comment that I really work out "hard", I calmly responded:

"Can't you see? I'm doing lip exercises!"

Think Positively

You need to be a positive and cheerful person to use humor. Avoid things that influence you negatively, such as latest news or negative people. There are people who always see the negative side in things and you definitely don't need them. Instead, look for positive people and spend time with them.

What you need to know is that everything around you contributes to shaping your personality. TV, websites, your friends, and acquaintances – they all influence you in a certain way, so you should make sure that they influence you positively. Make sure to be exposed to humor, watch comedies, read funny stories and spend time with funny people.

Chapter 10 – How to Handle Difficult Conversations

When there is a need for a difficult conversation, you simply feel it. Your gut tells you that a conflict occurred and it needs to be resolved as soon as possible. Otherwise, you and everyone else involved might face bigger consequences, such as your relationship breaking down or your company not achieving expected results.

Unfortunately, it's not easy to start and handle a difficult conversation. It's probably natural that most of us don't like uncomfortable conversations and often put the difficult discussion off for another time. In the meantime, the conflict rises and you and people around you all suffer.

There are different reasons for a disagreement between people. If you are at work, it can be that your project failed and you went into an argument with other co-workers on who's to blame. Perhaps your love partner didn't approve of something that you had done. Or you were simply nervous and snapped at your friend for no reason.

Either way, a difficult conversation is required to fix the relationship. The main thing that you need to have to start is courage. The good news is that the more experienced you get at these conversations; it will be easier for you to lead them.

Here are some conversation tactics that can serve as guidelines for approaching an important conversation properly:

Analyze the Problem

Before you start the conversation, carefully analyze the problem that set the conflict in motion. You need to detect the exact behavior that is causing the conflict. In other words, you need to know to explain what's wrong with a couple of clear and precise sentences. If you are bothered with your co-worker missing deadlines, explain how that behavior is influencing you, the rest of your team and the company itself. Keep focus and don't stray off-topic. It is pretty easy to stray during a conversation and worsen things by talking about essential unimportant issues.

Know Your Goals

Find out what do you expect from the conversation. Think about the outcome you want to achieve. If your co-worker is missing the deadlines, you will need him to agree that he won't do that anymore. Why was he missing them in the first place? Can you maybe help him finish his work on time?

The idea is to finish the conversation with an agreement on the steps that you will both take to repair the issue. You can also think about scheduling another conversation in a couple of weeks to see if the issue has been solved.

How Do You Feel About the Situation?

Before having a difficult conversation with the other party, have a conversation with yourself. Try figuring out how the other party makes you feel and try to anticipate possible responses you will get during the discussion.

Ask Questions

You might think that the situation is clear, but a proper approach to conversation also means that you should allow the other side to have an opinion. When starting a conversation, make sure to hear the other part of the story. Also, don't reject the story of the other party as nonsense before you analyze it.

Leave Your Emotions at Home

During a difficult conversation, you need to try to steer clear of emotional and irrational reactions as much as possible. If you want to handle and lead a difficult conversation, it's essential to manage your emotions. The other party might annoy you with what they are saying, but you should try to peacefully accept their responses. Otherwise, the conversation might escalate into something much serious, such as anger or rage. Keep in mind that you need to keep both and the other party's dignities. You don't have to agree with your conversation partner, but you have to show them some respect.

You should also know that the other side might have different emotional reactions. For example, they might cry. In this case, it is advised not to ignore their tears. Instead, offer them a tissue and a couple of seconds to gather their thoughts.

Silence Is Not a Bad Thing

Moments of silence in difficult conversations are there for a reason. Sometimes you need a couple of seconds to think about what was said up to that point in the discussion. If you let the message sink in, you will have a better idea how to continue from there. Aside from that, silence will calm all parties participating in the conversation.

If you are an outgoing person, it might be hard for you to get used to silences. It is because you are used to thinking while you are talking. Not all persons are like that. Introvert people like to think through before they say anything. You need to allow a couple of seconds and let them share their opinion. It will help resolving a conflict and coming up with a solution.

Choose the Right Place and Moment for the Conversation

A good idea is to strike up a conversation when you are alone with the other party. Also, make sure that you have enough time for a conversation. You don't want anybody to interrupt you in the middle of the discussion and prevent you from finishing it.

If you are a superior and you need to resolve a conflict with your employee, it might not be a good idea to call him to your office. The reason is that your office is considered your turf. What you want for a difficult conversation is a neutral location. It can be a meeting room or a coffee. The important thing is that you both feel comfortable in that place.

How to Inform Someone That You Need to Have a Difficult Talk with Them?

As I already mentioned, it might be the hardest to start a difficult discussion. It's not much easier to let them know that you need to talk. Experts suggest that there is no need to beat around the bush. Instead, use a simple and direct approach.

"Steve, I want to talk to you about what our boss told this

morning in the meeting about missing deadlines. Can we go to the coffee shop after work to talk?"

Alternatively, you can also say:

"Steve, I'm worried about the problem of missing deadlines our boss emphasized this morning. I want to help solve this issue. Can we go to the coffee shop to talk?"

You owe the other party to be sincere in your approach. Don't ambush them and say something like:

"Hey, the weather is so nice today! Let's go to the coffee shop for a drink!"

You don't want to surprise them as it can damage your relationship. Plus, it can annoy them and they might be in a bad mood for a difficult conversation. Instead, you want to clearly let them know the nature of your chat. Emphasize that you believe a conversation will help to fix the issue and that you want to resolve any conflicts that occurred.

Chapter 11 – Workplace Conversation Tactics

I'm sure you were in a situation that you provide hard work and great results for years, yet you are somehow overlooked for a promotion. The truth is that office politics are just as important as the work you deliver. If anything, fulfilling the actual job assignments might be even less important than improving your reputation around the office through office relationships and politics.

Conversation tactics I offer in this chapter will help you get up the office ladder and improve relationships with your co-workers.

Praise Your Co-Workers

Compliments also work in an office environment. In fact, they are the best way to strengthen the bond with your co-workers.

The truth is that we all love paydays. Financial payoff is one of the things that motivate us to get up from our beds and go to work every day. However, would you be surprised if I tell you that it's not the most important thing on the list?

According to many studies over the last several years, acknowledgment, validation, and recognition mean more to people than the financial payoff. This might be a great advice for managers as compliments are free and they are a great way of keeping your employer happy.

Pay attention to what your co-workers are doing well and

compliment them on it. Especially validate them in front of other people in your office. Do it every day and don't wait for special occasions. You will notice that they will soon start to compliment you back.

Ask for Help

You know how you sometimes look for a co-worker to get help from them? More often than not, they will actually help you and get that current problem of your chest. There are a couple of tricks you can apply to increase the chances that they will agree to help you.

The first thing to make sure is that you present your problem like an easily solvable one.

"Steve, I only need 10 minutes of your time. I will come to your office and bring coffee. Sugar or cream?"

When somebody asks you for help this way, it's hard to say no. Another thing that might help is to show your co-worker that you really tried but just failed to find a solution. If you say that you've conducted your own research and you just need to fill in a couple of blanks, anybody will be happy to guide you. After all, this way you will also acknowledge that you value that co-worker and you appreciate his/her skills.

Offer Help

People often look to solve their own problems neglecting that others might also be facing some issues in completing their daily assignments. If a co-worker ask you for help and it doesn't require a lot of your time (or they ask you nicely), there is no reason to turn them down. Agreeing to help will only strengthen the bond and bring you closer together.

Some co-workers are pretty shy and they might beat around

the bush to see if you are willing to help them. Make sure to stay in the moment and listen carefully what they have to say. It will enable you to see that they are trying to ask you for help. If you offer your assistance by yourself, you will score additional points with them.

Take Notes

Each employee in the office should have their own notebook. It's something that will help you keep track of your current assignments, projects, comments or questions you need to address. There is no chance that you can keep it all in your head.

As for how a notebook can help you with improving your relationship with co-workers, it's pretty simple. When a co-worker is talking about a current assignment (or anything else you consider important), take out your notebook and write down what they have to say. This will give them a feeling that they are important. There is no better way to validate them than to show them their words are so important that you have to write them down not to forget them. Of course, be careful as not everything is actually worth writing down.

Don't Be a Suck-Up

Somebody from your office just got a new idea. Regardless of who it is, whether it's your superior or a co-worker, suck-ups will immediately comment something like:

"Wow, that's a brilliant idea!"

Experienced personnel will immediately figure out that they are just agreeing to score some points. That's why you want to go down a different road – the path of meaningful feedback.

Be tactful and start by asking something like:

"How did you come up with that?"

"Do you think that's the best way to go?"

"What about this other method that…"

The idea is to offer useful information or challenge them to better articulate their thoughts. If they reassure you that that is the way to go then you should agree with them!

Managers, especially those who are experienced at this job, appreciate feedback and different opinions. Of course, you should be careful to share your opinion with respect towards everyone participating in the conversation. And if you offered an alternate approach and finally agreed that the first one offered by them is the best way to go, they will have a feeling that they've convinced you. This is also both a way of validating them and letting them see that you can listen to logic.

Chapter 12 – What Can You Learn from Leaders?

Leaders are people that lead their team through thick and thin and help them achieve business objectives and exceed expectations. Although a term "born leader" is often mentioned, that is far from the truth. Leaders are not born, they try hard to excel at certain skills and it takes a lot of time for a person to become a leader.

Among other things, leaders also need to have likable and approachable personalities. Knowledge of proper communication with people in their surroundings is an essential trait of every leader. That is why we can definitely learn a lot on how to become a conversation master from leaders.

Leaders apply conversation tactics every day and each time they communicate with someone.

The Characteristics of a Leader:

- **Confidence**

Leaders can't afford to be unsure in anything they say or do. They are aware that they are in charge of entire teams. If they are unsure of their words, it will reflect all other people in their team and negatively influence their confidence.

Of course, leaders aren't prone to emotions. Some of them will admit that they are afraid of speaking in front of a room full of people or scared that the project won't go the way they planned. However, great leaders will look like they are confident even when things go bad.

Confidence is built with practice. The first thing that you need to get out of your brain is negative thinking, such as:

"I don't have anything interesting to say to these people."

Always try to engage in as many social situations as possible. Your network of contacts will expand with time and your confidence will rise accordingly. As it happens, more people will be attracted to initiate the conversation with you first.

- **Honesty**

A good leader will always let you know the real situation, regardless of how bad it can look. A leader must be honest with his team in every moment, when things are going great and when the team is going through a rough patch.

Why do the leaders do that? Because they want people to trust them. By being honest with their team members, they deserve their trust.

Honesty is also an advantage in any social situation. As we discussed earlier in the book, this doesn't mean that you should tell people everything that comes to your mind. It simply means that you shouldn't beat around the bush trying to tell what you think the other person wants to hear. Instead, be direct and build and cultivate an honest relationship with people from your surroundings.

- **Commitment**

Leaders always make sure to act in a way that will ensure him and his team to reach their goals. If the leader of your team promises you that you will get a bonus if you reach the objective earlier than expected, they should make sure to commit and fulfill their word.

It's the exact same way you should act in social interactions. Be true to your word and don't say stuff you don't really mean. If you offer your assistance to somebody or you promise that you will come to a certain event, make sure to fulfill your promise. Don't disappoint your co-worker and leave him hanging because you just didn't feel like helping him. It will backfire sooner than you think. Word of mouth spreads around quickly and soon nobody in the office will see you as trustworthy or likable.

- **Creativity**

Coming up with innovative and unique solutions is what makes a leader great. Creativity is a personality trait held in high regards by most people because all of us appreciate new ideas and creative thoughts.

Be creative during your social interactions. Instead of having a boring chit-chat with your co-worker, put a twist into it and suggest some unusual topics. Aside from asking him dozens of questions about his current project, ask him about the last time he went to the movies or start a talk about his children.

- **Clear Communication**

Leaders always know how to say what they mean in a clear and concise way. If you have a leader in your team or you simply have a friend that has his own team, pay attention to how they are communicating. You will notice that they use conversation tactics offered in this book.

They have proper body posture, they speak directly by addressing people with their names and they properly articulate what they have to say while maintaining eye contact. Leaders don't feel any anxiety which is something they learned with experience. If you often engage in social interactions, you will notice that you will also be relieved of any anxiety when it comes to talking with other people.

- **Positive Attitude**

The team might be going through a rough patch, but a reliable leader will never let something like that get to him. They will make sure to learn what they can from a negative period and make sure something like that doesn't happen ever again. Leaders are always positive and believe that everything will have a positive outcome.

Once again, we see that leaders have arrived at such a high position on the business ladder because they've become conversation masters. Like I mentioned before, people like to surround themselves with cheerful and positive people. The best way to find your positivity is to focus on the positive traits you have. We all have our qualities and flaws, so focus on what's best when it comes to you. Once you develop a positive attitude about yourself, it will be much easier to be positive when communicating with other people.

- **Enthusiasm and Inspiration**

A leader not only has to come up with their own idea. They also need to present their ideas in a way that will make their team follow them. A sure way to do this is to display enthusiasm about the idea. This will inspire team members to accept the new idea and start applying it in current and future projects.

Enthusiasm is also important in social interactions. You need to be in the moment and be present in every conversation. Don't wander around the room with your eyes and pay attention to what the other party has to say. Show some enthusiasm by giving a sincere compliment about a certain detail related to your conversation partner.

Chapter 13 – Love-life Conversation Tactics

You might have an amazing relationship with your partner. However, it doesn't matter how great the relationship is, some degree of conflict is bound to show up sooner or later. When this happens, it is essential to resolve it as soon as possible. Otherwise, it might lead to more serious problems and maybe even the end of the relationship.

There are two wrong ways to react if you come into conflict with your partner:

- Responding to criticism with criticism. This can lead to very ugly arguments that you definitely don't need
- Avoiding the conflict completely

You might be on different pages when it comes to issues like finances, health habits, household tasks or having children. Either way, you need to have a difficult conversation to resolve the issue as soon as possible. Fortunately, there are conversation tactics that focus strictly on difficult conversations you have with your love partner.

You Don't Have to Be Right

You might think that this is a rule only for women, but the truth is that men love to be right just as much. Before you start a difficult conversation with your partner, make sure to clear this with yourself. There is no need for you to be right if it will help resolve the conflict. After all, does it really matter who is right and who is wrong? The important thing is that you repaired your relationship and that you are both eager to work together to improve things. So, be prepared to embrace different points of view and accept opinions that are different than yours.

Pick the Perfect Moment

You don't want to attack your partner as soon as they come back from work or if you see they are in a bad mood. You should choose the moment where you are both at your best. Also, make sure that you both have enough time for a long conversation. Consider agreeing in advance when you will have the discussion. Even if you do that, make sure to check again if that is a good time. If your partner feels like rescheduling, do that. On the other hand, if you feel like they are avoiding the conversation, remind them that it's in the best interest of your relationship to resolve the issue.

Start on a Positive Note

You might start by thanking your partner for agreeing to discuss the issue.

"Thanks for agreeing to talk to me. This thing has been bothering me for a while, but I already feel better knowing that you are willing to discuss and resolve the issue"

Listen Carefully

Aside from listening, make sure to actually hear and acknowledge what your partner has to say during the conversation. Refrain from interrupting them and don't think about your reply while your partner is in the middle of their talk. Stay in the moment and acknowledge the other party's comments before you respond.

A good way to show your partner that you have been listening carefully is to is to reflect back on what they've just said.

"So, let me see if I understood correctly what you were telling me…"

This conversation tactic is also called "reflective listening" and you can use it whenever your partner gets too upset or excited to calm the situation down.

Don't Stray Off-Topic

You've surely had your fair share of ups and downs in your relationship. However, discussion about resolving the conflict at hand is not a good moment to remind your partner about something that happened in ancient history. Even if your partner tries to steer the conversation in another direction, bring him back by simply saying:

"Let's focus on the issue at hand, please."

Play It Fair

Avoid accusing your partner that they're avoiding the issue or that they're to blame for the problem. It doesn't matter who is to blame as accusations always lead to bigger arguments. Your partner may counterattack and you will destroy all the progress you've made in just a couple of seconds.

Look for Things to Agree On

You might have a completely opposite stance on the issue than your partner. In this cases, look for small things to agree on as little consensus can go a long way in these situations.

Let's take a look at an example.

Your partner: "I want to have kids right now!"

You: "I agree that having kids is an important part of our relationship. I want them, too. I just think that we should buy a bigger place first."

Postpone the Discussion

Love-life conversation can get too difficult at times. In these cases, things get too heated and it seems that the issue cannot be resolved. Experts advise taking a small time-out if this happens. Schedule when you want to continue the conversation and make sure that the next discussion occurs as soon as possible (within 24 hours, if possible).

A little break will allow you both to calm yourselves down and you will be able to try to resolve the conflict once again. If the problem still persists, consider seeing a therapist or another professional.

Chapter 14 – PRACTICE: Exercise for Increasing Conversation Confidence

As I mentioned throughout the book – the more you engage in conversations, the more experienced you will become and it will give you more confidence.

Let me show you two conversation exercises that are an exciting and fun way to boost your confidence that you can discuss pretty much any topic.

Random Topic Selection

The first conversation exercises I will share with you can be done both by yourself and with your friends (as many people as you want can play the game).

The first thing you need to do is to write down around 20 conversation topics on separate pieces of paper. You can choose as many topics as you like, but I suggest using 20 in order to keep the exercise from lasting too long.

Here are some suggestions for the topics: Sports, Music, Passions, Movies, TV Shows, Relationships and Dating, Family, Marriage and Children, Hobbies, Vacation, Travel, Leisure Time, Adventure, Holiday, Food, Clothing and Fashion, something that you are wearing at the moment, Books, Social Life, Gossip, Current Events, Spirituality…

You can be as creative as you want with the topics, but try to use those that have the chance of coming up when you engage in social interactions.

Fold pieces of paper in a way that you can't see the topics and place them in a bowl.

Now, randomly pick a piece of paper, read the topic, set the timer to 20 seconds and try to speak about the topic given. When the timer counts down to zero, it's your partner's turn to select a topic. Alternatively, if you are exercising alone, all you have to do is pick up the next piece of paper.

When you see that 20 seconds is not enough time for what you have to say, feel free to increase the time. A recommended maximum is 60 seconds, although you can go longer if you think it's useful. Keep in mind that it's much better to shuffle the topics more often.

The benefits of this exercise include:

- You will get better at talking for longer period of times
- You will increase your conversation confidence
- You will improve your intuitive thinking
- It will be much easier to bring up memories

Keep in mind that it is much better to play in a company. The reason is simple – you will have to speak in front of an audience and you will increase your confidence more quickly.

The Last Word of the Story

The other conversation exercise can be played by only two people. The goal of the exercises is to tell a story together.

It's simple – one of the two people playing starts a story. He only tells a sentence or two and doesn't talk for more than 5-10 seconds. When he finishes, the other person playing needs to use the last word from the previous sentence to start their own story.

Let's see an example:

You: "I went to the mall last weekend and did some shopping!"

Your partner: "Shopping is my favorite way of spending free time!"

You: "Time is of the essence when you need to arrive at a class like I had to yesterday!"

Friend: "Yesterday I bought some potatoes and tomatoes!"

And so on...

Feel free to get creative, but the idea is to share your own experiences. The reason why you need to talk what really happened to you is because honesty is an important conversation tactic.

As for the exercises, it will train your brain to think more quickly and come up with similar stories to the ones your conversation partner is telling.

Conclusion

Thank you again for having this book!

I hope this book was able to help you see how it is more than possible to become an expert in starting and leading any conversation.

The next step is to be persistent and follow the tips described in this book. Remember, it's all in the experience and practice. The more you engage in social interactions, the better your social skills will become.

Soon, you won't be able to recognize yourself. You won't be shy anymore, you will approach strangers with ease and you will become a sociable person that everybody likes.

Finally, if you enjoyed this book, then I'd like to ask you for a favor, would you be kind enough to leave a review for this book on Amazon? It'd be greatly appreciated.

I would like to know your feedback; you can review this book on Amazon!

Thank you and good luck!

Preview of "Minimalist Living" Book

Introduction

This book contains proven steps and strategies on minimalist living.

Do you feel like your cluttered home makes you more stressful than comfortable? Do you think that you don't have time to dedicate yourself to things that are important to you? Does it seem like things and unnecessary distractions are running your life instead of you?

I've had the exact same issues like you and I can assure you, becoming a minimalist is an excellent way of regaining control over your life. The great news is that there is no strict rule or a line of becoming a minimalist.

Minimalism is a philosophy of focusing on only the essential things. A minimalistic approach means that you are not cluttering your life with unnecessary things and that you have simplified it as much as possible. Each person is free to decide their own limits in adopting minimalism. One thing is certain – becoming a minimalist will make you feel better, happier and healthier in no time!

I've been living as a minimalist for years now and it feels great. That is why I've decided to share my experience and offer valuable insights and tips on how to adopt a minimalistic approach to life.

The book is anything but theory. I tried to focus on practical tips and benefits of minimalizing your life in different areas. We will cover various issues, such as:

- How to declutter your home and get rid of all unneeded things easily?
- How to get rid of all extra clothes and how to shop for new ones like a minimalist?
- How to travel and move around to maximize enjoyment of every moment of life?
- How to use the technology the help you become a minimalist and unclutter your digital environment?

And much more!

I've used my own and experience of other true minimalists to help you on your path to becoming a part of our group and start leading a stress-free and happy life!

Thanks again for downloading this book, I hope you enjoy it!

Chapter 1 – How to Simplify Your Life

There's something special in simplicity. It brings feelings of balance and freedom. Living as a minimalist is a guarantee that you will have a simpler life. You will not only have more time and space; you will also have a decluttered mind free of all stressful thinking.

Why Should You Become a Minimalist?

Before we move on to the tips on how to simplify your life, let's take a look at some reasons why you should become a minimalist:

- **You will be friendlier** – freeing up your time will give you more opportunities to think about how you treat people. You will become a better listener and start giving more attention to details
- **You will appreciate the silence** – you might think that you need speed and pressure in your life, but once you see stop for just a second, you will learn to appreciate solitude and silence.
- **You will make better decisions** – we are constantly faced with making choices. Minimalist living will decrease the amount of decisions you need to make, enabling you to focus on the important ones
- **You will have a healthier lifestyle** – minimalist way of life allows you to pay attention to your lifestyle. Soon, you will find yourself avoiding junk food and adopting a healthier way of living.
- **You will improve your self-confidence** – you can focus on things that are most important to you. That will enable you to get your life in line with your values, which will raise your self-confidence
- **You are ready for changes** – if you live with less, you make yourself more adaptable to changes. It's much easier to make simpler transitions and accept both small and bigger changes.
- **You will feel less stressed** – as I mentioned, mental decluttering is equally important as physical.

Relaxed and relieved state of mind will help you improve your personality and act better as a human

9 Important Things to Do to Make Your Life Simpler

Possessions

You can't even begin to think how too many material possessions can complicate your life. Your bank account gets drained quickly, as well as your energy level. Material possessions are what keep us from our loved ones and the life we want to live. Investing time in removing material possession you don't really need will be the best decision you have ever made.

Commitments

I assume that you have an endless list of commitments every day. It starts from work, continues with chores and kids' activities and ends in community events and other endeavors. Think about what you value the most and make room only for the things you feel should be a priority.

Goals

You don't need more than one or two goals at any moment of your life. That will improve your focus and increase your success rate. A good idea is to make a list of all the things you want in your life. Next, select two goals you consider a top priority. Don't include any other goals until you finish at least one of these two.

Negative Thinking

Negative thoughts are no good, except to add to your bitterness, resentment or hate. You don't want to feel these emotions. Instead, try to take responsibility for what you think. Make your mind forgive for what happened in the past and focus on positive thinking about the present and future

Finances

Start reducing your debt today, even if it's just for a little amount. Try hard and start pulling out of debt. If you need, look for help from your friends. Get rid of all luxurious things today in order to enjoy tomorrow.

Try not to worry about credit card debt, student loans or medical bills. Instead, sit down and realistically analyze your financial situation. What are your incomes and what are your expenses? What is the amount of debt you have to pay? Try to find a way to spend as little as possible on groceries and other basics. Have a plan for each cent of your money and you will easily get your finances in order and simplify your life.

Nutrition

The main thing you want to do is avoid artificial ingredients, such as refined grain (yes, that's white bread), trans fats, and sodium. Reducing the intake of bad ingredients will both help with your energy levels and your health. Another thing to avoid are over-the-counter medicines. Try to allow your body to heal itself naturally whenever possible.

Technology

Limit the use of technology. Avoid video games, television, movies and other media. You would be surprised how easy it can start dominating your life and having great impact on your values and attitude.

You should also set a limit when it comes to using social media and your smartphone. Yes, it is an important thing to keep in touch with other people and cultivate relationships, but you don't want to get distracted all the time as your mind can easily drift and you won't be able to focus on important things.

Check Out My Other Books

Below you'll find some of my other popular books that are popular on Amazon and Kindle as well. Simply click on the links below to check them out. Alternatively, you can visit my "Author Page" on Amazon to see other work done by me: **Anas Malla**: http://amzn.to/2nzCevB

- **Minimalist Living**
  http://amzn.to/2phTu8M

- **Ketogenic Bread Cookbook**
  http://amzn.to/2m8hixm

If the links do not work, for whatever reason, you can simply search for these titles on the Amazon website to find them.

CPSIA information can be obtained
at www.ICGtesting.com
Printed in the USA
LVHW080014110419
613755LV00036B/1040/P

9 781545 301104